THE
healthy heart
COOKBOOK

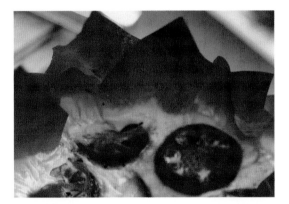

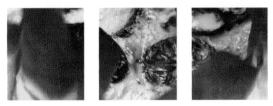

DAWN STOCK

p

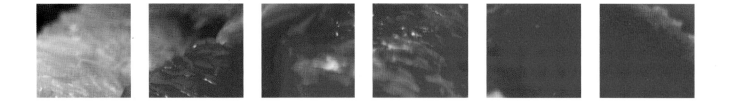

This is a Parragon Book
This edition published in 2005

Parragon
Queen Street House
4 Queen Street
Bath
BA1 1HE
UK

Designed and produced by
THE BRIDGEWATER BOOK COMPANY

Nutritional Facts and Analyses: *Charlotte Watts*
Photography: *Clive Bozzard-Hill*
Home economist: *Phillipa Vanstone*
Stylist: *Angela Macfarlane*

The publishers would like to thank the following companies for the loan
of props: *Dartington Crystal, Marlux Mills, Maxwell & Williams, Lifestyle Collections,
Viners & Oneida, Typhoon and John Lewis.*

Printed in China

ISBN: 1-40544-584-X

NOTES FOR THE READER

This book uses metric and imperial measurements. Follow the same units
of measurement throughout; do not mix metric and imperial. All spoon
measurements are level, unless otherwise stated: teaspoons are assumed
to be 5 ml and tablespoons are assumed to be 15 ml.

Individual vegetables such as potatoes are medium and pepper is freshly
ground black pepper. Salt is not included in the recipes and should only
be added to foods at the table where absolutely necessary. Milk used in the
recipes is skimmed or semi-skimmed to help limit the fat content of the meal.
The recipes have been made with a reduced-fat and -sugar content in
accordance with healthy eating guidelines. However, this means that they
will not keep fresh for as long a period of time as their higher-fat and -sugar
alternatives. This is particularly the case with cakes, so storage advice has
been included where appropriate.

Some of the recipes require stock. If you use commercially made stock
granules or cubes, these can have a relatively high salt content, so do not
add any further salt. If you make your own stock, keep the fat and salt content
to a minimum. Don't fry the vegetables before simmering – just simmer the
vegetables, herbs and meat, poultry or fish in water and strain. Meat and
poultry stocks should be strained, cooled and refrigerated before use so that
the fat from the meat rises to the top and solidifies – it can then be easily
removed and this reduces the saturated fat content of the meal. Homemade
stocks should be stored in the refrigerator and used within two days, or frozen
in usable portions and labelled.

The values of the nutritional analysis for each recipe refer to a single
serving, or a single slice where relevant. They do not include the serving
suggestion. Where a range of portions is given the nutritional analysis figure
refers to the mid-range figure. The calorific value given is in KCal (Kilocalories).
The carbohydrate figure includes starches and sugars, with the sugar value
then given separately. The fat figure is likewise the total fat, with the saturated
part then given separately.

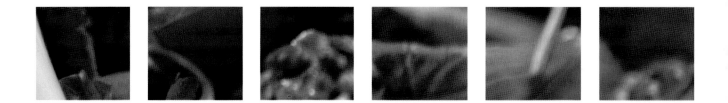

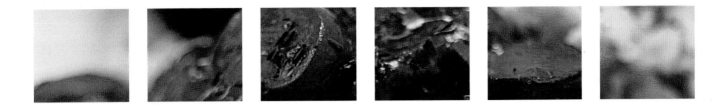

contents

Introduction

We spend a lot of time and money looking after our outward appearance and increasingly feel the need to halt the signs of ageing, for instance, by concealing our grey hairs or applying anti-wrinkle creams to our skins. However, we often don't pay nearly the same amount of attention to the condition of our internal organs – the heart in particular. Given its fundamental importance to our entire well-being, we really should take time to think about our heart's state of health and its day-to-day maintenance.

Diet and Exercise Caution

Before embarking on any diet, you should consult your doctor, especially if you have recently been ill or have special dietary or medical requirements, or if you are pregnant or breastfeeding, are a child or are elderly.

Before taking up any exercise programme, you should consult your doctor, especially if you are worried about any aspect of your health, particularly if you suffer from respiratory problems such as asthma or bronchitis, or suffer from heart disease, high blood pressure, back trouble, joint pains or arthritis, or if you have recently had an operation or been ill.

The trend in the UK is for an increasing number of people to be overweight. We are eating a diet that is increasingly higher in fat, sugars and salts and engaging in less exercise. If we add stress, smoking and excessive drinking to this lifestyle, we are undoubtedly putting extra strain on our bodies and our hearts.

But it's never too late to start looking after yourself. The recipes in this cookbook show you how to adopt a healthy eating lifestyle, by reducing the saturated fat, sugar and salt and increasing the fruit, vegetables and fibre in your diet, in simple and appetising ways. Even if you only pick up a few of the practical dietary messages in this cookbook, you will enjoy the benefits – including the pleasure of eating great food!

We all have good days and bad days. If you have a meal out to celebrate a special occasion that is high in calories and full of fat, don't give up in despair – just be more careful about what you eat for the next few days. Just remember that your healthy eating meals should outnumber the excessive, indulgent ones.

Reduce Your Risk

You can reduce your risk of coronary heart disease by:

• Not being overweight.
• Eating less saturated fat.
• Eating five portions of fruit and vegetables a day.
• Eating fewer salty snacks and by not adding salt to your food.
• Eating fewer sugary snacks and drinks.
• Drinking moderate amounts of alcohol and not exceeding the recommended guidelines regularly.
• Not smoking.
• Exercising regularly – three hours of cardiovascular exercise per week is recommended.
• Reducing your stress levels and learning to relax.
• Eating a healthy diet, which can help to balance and reduce harmful cholesterol levels.

Eating a balanced, healthy diet may help reduce your risk of coronary heart disease and benefit you by:

• Helping you to reach or maintain a healthy body weight and so reduce the strain on your heart.
• Helping you to lower your blood cholesterol level.
• Keeping your blood pressure down.
• Helping to prevent the unwanted fatty layer from building up in the inside walls of your arteries, which, over time, can restrict blood flow.
• Helping to prevent blood clots called thrombosis forming. Thrombosis can ultimately cause heart attacks and strokes.
• Increasing your chances of survival if you do suffer a heart attack.

Hard Heart Facts

Coronary heart disease is a major cause of death and illness in the UK and accounts for 120,000 deaths each year. This means that one in four men and one in six women now die from this disease. Women should not be complacent – there are concerns that they may be placing themselves at a greater risk as increasing numbers of younger women are eating unhealthily, drinking more alcohol, smoking and exercising less.

Some factors that increase our risk of heart disease cannot be influenced, for example, if there is a family history of heart disease or if you have diabetes. Another contributory factor over which we have no control is ageing. However, we can all help reduce our risk of heart disease by eating a healthy diet, exercising more and stopping smoking.

Eat Your Way to a Healthy Heart

By following these simple guidelines, you will improve your diet and help to look after your heart.

Reduce Excess Weight

There is no question that being overweight puts a strain on your entire body since it has to work harder to carry you about, putting a strain on your joints, organs and especially your heart. Being overweight can also increase your risk of high blood pressure and can unbalance the ratio of good to bad cholesterol in the blood and therefore increase your risk of coronary heart disease. Reducing the fat in your diet is a good starting point to losing excess weight, but remember to consult a doctor before starting any diet programme. If you don't need to lose weight but you plan to reduce the amount of fat in your diet, you will need to replace these lost calories by eating more starchy foods – see page 8 for advice.

Eat Fewer Saturated and Trans Fats

Although a small amount of fat is needed in our diet to provide essential vitamins and fatty acids that our bodies cannot alone provide, most people need to reduce the amount of saturated fat that they eat. It is important to understand about the different fats we eat in our foods, so that we can make healthier food choices. There are two types of fat in the diet: saturated and unsaturated. The unsaturated fats include polyunsaturated and monounsaturated fats.

Saturated fats are the fats we should be eating less of because they raise blood cholesterol levels more than anything else in the diet, which in turn encourages the development of fatty deposits in the walls of the arteries and can cause the blood to thicken and clot. Narrowing arteries and clots (also called thrombus) can, over time, restrict the flow of blood and result in a heart attack or stroke. Saturated fats are found mainly in dairy products such as butter, cheese, yogurt, fromage frais,

The Cholesterol Conundrum

Cholesterol occurs naturally in the body and plays a vital role in how every cell wall in the body functions. However, too much cholesterol in the blood can increase the risk of coronary heart disease. Nearly half of all deaths from coronary heart disease in the UK are due to raised cholesterol levels in the blood, therefore it is very important to eat healthily. Cholesterol is carried around the body in the blood on proteins called lipoproteins. A healthy body should have low levels of 'bad' cholesterol (called LDL, or low-density lipoproteins) and higher levels of 'good' cholesterol (called HDL, or high-density lipoproteins), as this appears to protect against coronary heart disease by removing excess cholesterol from the blood. Reducing the saturated fat content of the diet is now considered far more important than cutting down on foods in which cholesterol can be found, such as eggs, liver and kidneys, as a way of preventing and controlling high cholesterol levels in the blood.

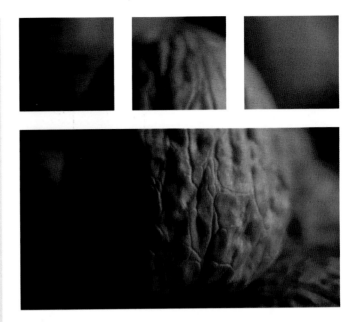

cream, milk and meat. They are also found in a few vegetable oils such as coconut and palm oil, hard margarines and lard, and are 'hidden' in processed foods like biscuits, cakes and chocolate.

Unsaturated fats can be either polyunsaturated or monounsaturated, and both play an important role in a healthy diet to replace saturated oils and help to reduce blood cholesterol levels. There are two types of polyunsaturated fats. The first is found in the seeds of plants such as the sunflower and soya oil and is called omega-6. The second type comes mainly from oily fish and is called omega-3 (see page 9). Monounsaturated fats have been found to lower the amount of bad cholesterol in the blood, so they help to maintain a healthy balance of cholesterol in the body. Monounsaturated fats can be found mainly in olive oil, avocados and nuts, all of which have been used in the recipes in the book. Recipes that are traditionally high in fat have been made with a reduced-fat content and saturated fats have been replaced with polyunsaturated or monounsaturated fats where possible.

How to Reduce Fat Intake

The recipes in the book illustrate the following ways in which you can reduce the amount of saturated fat in your diet:

1. Cut off all visible fat from meats and poultry and remove and discard any skin.
2. Use low-fat rather than full-fat forms of natural yogurt, fromage frais, cottage cheese and quark.
3. Don't fry foods in butter or lard – try to avoid frying foods altogether. If you have to sauté foods, use olive or sunflower oil instead and as little of it as possible.
4. Use skimmed or semi-skimmed milk.
5. Use sauces made only with cornflour as the thickener rather than using the traditional roux (butter and flour) method. Add flavour by using herbs, spices and other ingredients such as fruit rind and juice.
6. Use healthier, low-fat cooking methods such as grilling and simmering rather than deep-frying.
7. Use low-fat salad dressings instead of high-fat salad creams and mayonnaise.
8. Replace butter with a spread labelled high in polyunsaturates such as sunflower spread.

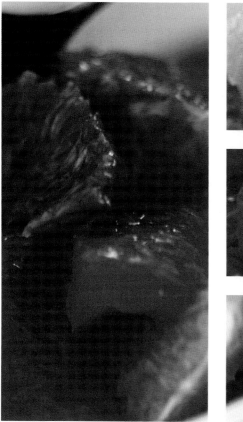
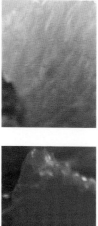

Eat More Starch and Fibre

Healthy eating recommendations advise us all to eat more starchy foods and fibre. Insoluble fibre from cereals prevents constipation and enables the digestive tract to rid the body of waste, as well as stopping cholesterol being reabsorbed into the bloodstream. Soluble fibre from fruit, pulses and vegetables can help to reduce the amount of cholesterol in the blood. Therefore, it is important to eat a varied diet so that you get the benefits of both insoluble and soluble fibre.

Breads, potatoes, pasta and rice are starchy foods with a useful amount of fibre. These foods are good at filling us up, provide important nutrients and, because they take longer to digest, (particularly wholegrain foods) make us feel fuller for longer, which in turn can prevent us from snacking on high-fat and salty foods. If you are trying to lose weight, you should still include some starchy foods in your diet.

The recipes in this book recommend the use of brown rice, wholemeal bread and wholemeal flour. However, if you are not used to eating these, introduce them gradually into your diet. It is still better to eat more white bread, pasta and rice to replace the calories lost by reducing the fat content of your diet, and they provide useful amounts of protein, vitamins and minerals.

Eat More Fruit and Vegetables

Eating at least five portions of fruit and vegetables a day is recommended for a healthy diet and is also thought to help reduce the risk of coronary heart disease. In the UK, people are only eating an average of three portions a day, so this is an area of our health we can improve upon. Fruit and vegetables contain important antioxidants found in vitamins and these are believed to help prevent the thickening of the artery walls. Vitamins C and E are also thought to be good at aiding arterial repair. Apples, apricots, broccoli, carrots, all citrus fruits, kiwi fruit, mangoes, onions, peppers, potatoes and tomatoes are all good sources of antioxidants and have been used in many of the recipes in this book. Fruit and vegetables are also a good source of the mineral potassium, which is thought to help control blood pressure and prevent irregular heart rhythms. Bananas and potatoes are good sources of potassium and are featured in the recipes.

The Trans-fatty Acids Issue

Recently, there has been concern that the process called hydrogenation, in which various vegetable and animal oils are turned into solids to make margarine or spreads, leads to the formation of trans-fatty acids. These trans-fatty acids are treated in the body in the same way as saturated fats and so may raise the level of cholesterol in the diet if eaten in large quantities. Currently, we are advised to use a fat low in saturated fat and containing higher levels of polyunsaturated or monounsaturated fats. If possible, look carefully at the nutritional labelling and choose a product whose trans-fatty acids and saturated fat levels are less than 15 per cent. For recipes in the book that require a spread rather than an oil, use a sunflower spread labelled high in polyunsaturates.

How to Eat Five Portions a Day

Fresh, frozen or canned fruit and vegetables are all beneficial. Try to eat a wide selection of both fruit and vegetables. Remember that potatoes don't count as one of the five portions as they are considered a starchy food and that a glass of fruit juice counts as only one portion, no matter how much you drink. Using the recipes in this book will help you to reach the five portions a day quota. Plenty of fruit, vegetables and salads have been included either in the recipes or suggested as accompaniments to a meal.

How big is a portion? The list below gives a general idea of amounts required to constitute one portion:

- 1 apple, orange or banana.
- 2 plums, apricots, kiwi fruit or satsumas.
- A handful of grapes, strawberries or other small fruits.
- 2 tablespoons of vegetables.
- A small handful of dried fruit such as cranberries, raisins or sultanas.
- A dessert bowl of salad ingredients.
- A glass of fruit juice (about 150 ml/5 fl oz).

Eat More Fish

It has always been said that fish is good for you. Now, eating oily fish is actively being promoted as it is believed to play a vital role in reducing the risk of coronary heart disease. It is thought that eating oily fish may help to keep levels of the fatty substances in the blood called triglycerides down and so help prevent blood clots from forming in the arteries. Omega-3 is found in oily fish such as kippers, mackerel, tuna, salmon, sardines and pilchards. Recipes in this book such as Quick Mackerel Pâté (see page 38), Teriyaki Salmon Fillets with Chinese Noodles (see page 54), Grilled Tuna & Vegetable Kebabs (see page 51) and Kipper Kedgeree (see page 26) offer tasty ways in which to enjoy oily fish. It is recommended that we eat fish two to three times a week, of which one should be oily fish.

Eat Less Salt

A high consumption of salt in the diet is linked to high blood pressure. It is the sodium in salt that contributes to high blood pressure. The recommended maximum daily intake is 6 g but our bodies only need 1 g (about a good pinch!).

Most of us should try and reduce the amount of salt we eat. The recipes in this book have no salt added during the preparation or cooking of the dish. If, once you have tasted them, you feel that they need seasoning, add salt at the table and try to reduce the amount needed gradually. Your taste buds will soon become accustomed to a lower salt content. Herbs, spices, freshly ground black pepper and other ingredients such as lemon rind have been added to the dishes to create flavour instead of using salt. Remember if you are using manufactured foods that salt will have already been added, so try not to add any more! About three-quarters of the salt we eat comes from processed foods such as stock cubes, biscuits, ready-prepared meals and snacks.

Eat Less Sugar

Sugar provides calories alone and no essential nutrients, and healthy eating recommendations advise that most of us should be eating less sugar. Sugar that is not used for energy is converted into fat by the liver and stored, adding to obesity and heart disease risk. The recipes in this cookbook are low in added sugar and often use the natural sugars found in fruit such as apples and dried fruit to sweeten the food. Using fruit also helps to meet the recommended five-a-day fruit and vegetable portions and provides useful amounts of fibre, vitamins and minerals.

Drink Less Alcohol

Excessive alcohol consumption can increase blood pressure, damage the heart muscle and lead to unwanted weight gain as alcohol provides calories with no nutritional content. Drinking alcohol is also thought to cause the platelets in the blood to become stickier, making the blood thicker and thus hampering the blood's movement through the blood vessels. Although excessive drinking of alcohol is not recommended, drinking moderate amounts – 1–2 units of alcohol per day – may have a beneficial effect, particularly in men over 40 years of age and post-menopausal women. Pregnant women are advised not to drink any alcohol. Red wine has been found to have some beneficial effects as it is thought to increase the good cholesterol in the blood, which removes unwanted cholesterol and transports it to the liver for disposal. The quality of the wine must be good for this action to occur and for it to contain resveratrol, the antioxidant that has beneficial properties for the heart. One glass of wine, half a pint of average-strength beer or lager or one pub measure of spirits equals one unit of alcohol. So the advice is to enjoy a drink but don't overindulge.

Other Lifestyle Changes for a Healthy Heart

Reduce Stress: Learn to Relax and Exercise More

Continual stress is bad for your heart as it increases the level of adrenaline in the blood. This in turn makes the blood thicker and stickier and can eventually cause the arteries to narrow and thicken. Continual stress may also cause high blood pressure. Therefore, it is very important that you find time each day to relax and unwind. Exercising can be a good way to calm down and is also beneficial to your health. We should be doing three hours' exercise a week, such as a good brisk walk, swimming, cycling, dancing or playing a sport. Remember to take things gradually at first if you are not used to physical activity and consult a doctor if you have any health concerns before starting an exercise programme.

Stop Smoking

Smoking is bad for you, and you know it, so the best thing you can do for your health is to stop. Generally people who smoke cigarettes have twice the risk of having a heart attack than non-smokers since it contributes to the building up of fatty deposits in the arteries.

Reduce Your Risk

Remember – it is never too late to start caring for your heart and your health. The four most important steps you can take to help reduce your risk of coronary heart disease are:

1. Reduce your saturated and trans fat intake.
2. Exercise more.
3. Eat more fruit and vegetables.
4. Stop smoking.

Breakfasts & Brunches

Breakfast is the first and most important meal of the day. Eating a healthy breakfast kick-starts your metabolism, gives you energy and improves your concentration. Missing out on this meal can lead to hunger pangs and unhealthy high-fat and sugar-laden snacks later on. The recipes in this chapter include fast breakfasts for those who have to get up and go, as well as some ideas for more leisurely brunches for when you have time to treat yourself.

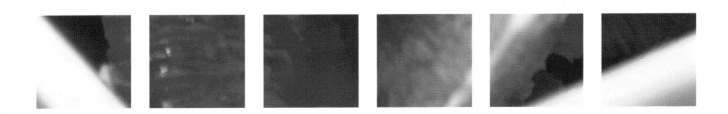

makes 10

Cranberry Muffins

Ingredients

175 g/6 oz self-raising white flour

55 g/2 oz self-raising wholemeal flour

1 tsp ground cinnamon

$^1/_2$ tsp bicarbonate of soda

1 egg, beaten

70 g/2$^1/_2$ oz thin-cut orange marmalade

150 ml/5 fl oz skimmed or semi-skimmed milk

5 tbsp sunflower oil

115 g/4 oz peeled, cored and finely diced dessert apple

115 g/4 oz fresh or frozen cranberries, thawed if frozen

1 tbsp porridge oats

freshly squeezed orange juice, to serve

1 Preheat the oven to 200°C/400°F/Gas Mark 6. Line a muffin tin with 10 muffin paper cases.

2 Put the two flours, cinnamon and bicarbonate of soda into a mixing bowl and combine thoroughly.

3 Make a well in the centre of the flour mixture. In a separate bowl, blend the egg with the marmalade until well combined. Beat the milk and oil into the egg mixture, then pour into the dry ingredients, stirring lightly. Do not over-mix – the mixture should be slightly lumpy. Quickly stir in the apple and cranberries.

4 Spoon the mixture evenly into the paper cases and sprinkle the oats over each muffin. Bake in the preheated oven for 20–25 minutes, or until well risen and golden, and a skewer inserted into the centre of a muffin comes out clean.

5 Lift out the muffins and transfer on to a wire rack. Leave for 5–10 minutes, or until slightly cooled. Peel off the paper cases and serve warm with glasses of freshly squeezed orange juice. These muffins are best eaten on the day they are made – any leftover muffins should be stored in an airtight container and consumed within 24 hours.

Nutritional Fact
Apples contain pectin, a type of fibre that is highly effective at removing toxins, which can damage the heart, from the body via the bowel.

Serving Analysis
- Calories   188
- Protein   4g
- Carbohydrate   25g
- Sugars   6.6g
- Fat   8.3g
- Saturates   1.4g

serves 1

Banana & Strawberry Smoothie

Ingredients

1 banana, sliced

85 g/3 oz fresh strawberries, hulled

150 g/5 1/2 oz low-fat natural yogurt

Nutritional Fact
Bananas contain potassium and strawberries contain antioxidants – both may help to protect the heart.

Serving Analysis
• Calories	169
• Protein	4.7g
• Carbohydrate	36.2g
• Sugars	30g
• Fat	1.95g
• Saturates	0.8g

1 Put the banana, strawberries and yogurt into a blender and process for a few seconds until smooth.

2 Pour into a glass and serve immediately.

serves 4

Exotic Dried Fruit Compote

Ingredients

115 g/4 oz no-soak dried peaches

85 g/3 oz no-soak dried apricots

55 g/2 oz no-soak dried pineapple chunks

55 g/2 oz no-soak dried mango slices

225 ml/8 fl oz unsweetened clear apple juice

4 tbsp low-fat natural yogurt (optional)

1 Put the dried fruit into a small saucepan with the apple juice. Bring slowly to the boil, then reduce the heat to low, cover and simmer for 10 minutes.

2 Spoon into serving dishes and top each serving with a tablespoon of yogurt, if desired. Serve immediately.

Nutritional Fact

The fruit content here provides a great amount of soluble fibre and therefore cleans out the bowel, which is very important for regulating cholesterol.

Serving Analysis

• Calories	165
• Protein	2g
• Carbohydrate	42g
• Sugars	36.6g
• Fat	0.49g
• Saturates	0.06g

serves 4

Bacon Buns

Ingredients

8 low-salt lean smoked back bacon rashers

6 tomatoes

250 g/9 oz low-fat natural cottage cheese

freshly ground black pepper

4 large seeded wholemeal or white bread rolls

2 spring onions, chopped

1 Preheat the grill to high. Remove any visible fat and rind from the bacon and cut 4 of the tomatoes in half. Place the bacon and tomatoes, cut-side up, under the preheated grill and cook, turning the bacon over halfway through cooking, for 8–10 minutes, or until the bacon is crisp and the tomatoes are softened. Remove the tomatoes and bacon from the grill and drain the bacon on kitchen paper to help remove any excess fat. Keep the bacon and tomatoes warm.

2 Meanwhile, cut the remaining tomatoes into bite-sized pieces and combine with the cottage cheese in a bowl. Cut the bacon into bite-sized pieces and stir into the cottage cheese mixture. Season to taste with pepper.

3 Cut the bread rolls in half and divide the bacon filling evenly over each roll base. Sprinkle the spring onions over the filling and cover with the roll tops. Serve immediately with the grilled tomatoes.

Nutritional Fact
Tomatoes contain a substance called lycopene, which gives them their lovely red colour and has great antioxidant and protective properties for the heart.

Serving Analysis
- *Calories* 216
- *Protein* 16g
- *Carbohydrate* 21.3g
- *Sugars* 7.2g
- *Fat* 8.2g
- *Saturates* 3.4g

serves 2

Melon & Kiwi Fruit Bowl

Ingredients

1 small Charentais, Cantaloupe or Galia melon

2 kiwi fruit

Nutritional Fact

Kiwi fruit is an excellent source of vitamin C, which is an antioxidant thought to play a key role in preventing heart disease.

Serving Analysis

- *Calories*   236
- *Protein*   3.25g
- *Carbohydrate*   54g
- *Sugars*   51g
- *Fat*   0.8g
- *Saturates*   0.14g

1 Cut the melon into quarters and remove and discard the seeds. Remove the melon flesh from the skin with a sharp knife and cut into chunks. If you have a melon baller, scoop out as much of the melon flesh as possible and place in a bowl.

2 Peel the kiwi fruit and cut the flesh into slices. Add to the melon and gently mix together. Cover and refrigerate until required or divide between 2 serving dishes and serve immediately.

serves 1

Rise & Shine Juice

Ingredients

4 tomatoes, quartered

85 g/3 oz grated carrot

1 tbsp lime juice

Nutritional Fact

Carrots contain high amounts of beta-carotene, which gives them their vibrant orange colour and their heart-protective properties.

Serving Analysis

• Calories	144
• Protein	5.1g
• Carbohydrate	33g
• Sugars	20g
• Fat	1.8g
• Saturates	0.25g

1 Put the tomatoes, carrot and lime juice into a blender and process for a few seconds until smooth.

2 Place a nylon sieve over a bowl and pour in the tomato mixture. Using a spoon, gently push as much of the liquid through the sieve as possible. Discard any pips and pulp remaining in the sieve.

3 Pour the juice into a glass and serve immediately.

serves 4

Kipper Kedgeree

Ingredients

1 tbsp olive oil

2 shallots, sliced

1 tsp ground cumin

1 tsp ground turmeric

400 g/14 oz easy-cook brown rice

700 ml/1¼ pints vegetable stock

2 eggs

115 g/4 oz frozen peas

4 spring onions, chopped

350 g/12 oz kipper fillets

freshly ground black pepper

2 tbsp chopped fresh parsley

lemon wedges, to garnish

Nutritional Fact

Kippers are an oily fish and so contain omega-3 oils that protect the heart. It is currently recommended that you eat 2–3 portions of fish per week, one of which should be oily.

Serving Analysis

• Calories	403
• Protein	29g
• Carbo	30g
• Sugars	2.8g
• Fat	18g
• Saturates	3.4g

1 Heat the oil in a large, heavy-based frying pan over a medium–low heat, add the shallots, cumin and turmeric and cook, stirring constantly, for 1–2 minutes, or until the shallots have softened, taking care not to burn the spices as they are cooking in a small amount of oil.

2 Add the rice and stir to coat with the oil and spices. Pour in the stock and bring to the boil, then reduce the heat, cover and simmer, stirring occasionally, for 25 minutes.

3 Meanwhile, place the eggs in a small saucepan of cold water and bring to the boil, then reduce the heat and simmer for 10 minutes. Carefully remove the eggs from the hot water and place in a bowl of cold water for a few minutes. When cool enough to handle, remove and discard the eggshells. Chop the eggs into bite-sized pieces and set aside.

4 Stir the peas and spring onions into the rice and return to the boil. Reduce the heat, cover and simmer for a further 5 minutes.

5 Using a sharp knife, remove and discard the skin from the kipper fillets. Cut the fish into bite-sized pieces, removing any remaining bones, and stir into the rice mixture. Return the rice to the boil, then reduce the heat, cover and simmer for 3–5 minutes, or until the fish is cooked, the rice is tender and the stock has been completely absorbed. Season to taste with pepper.

6 Transfer the kedgeree to a warmed serving dish and lightly fork in the eggs. Sprinkle over the parsley, garnish with lemon wedges and serve immediately.

serves 4

Citrus Zing

Ingredients

| 1 pink grapefruit |
| 1 yellow grapefruit |
| 3 oranges |

1 Using a sharp knife, carefully cut away all the peel and pith from the grapefruit and oranges.

2 Working over a bowl to catch the juice, carefully cut the grapefruit and orange segments between the membranes to obtain skinless segments of fruit. Discard any pips. Add the segments to the bowl and gently mix together. Cover and refrigerate until required or divide between 4 serving dishes and serve immediately.

Nutritional Fact
Citrus fruits are one of the highest sources of vitamin C, which is crucial for heart health as it is important for the healing of blood vessels.

Serving Analysis

- Calories   83
- Protein   1.6g
- Carbohydrate   21g
- Sugars   17g
- Fat   0.23g
- Saturates   0.03g

Soups & Light Meals

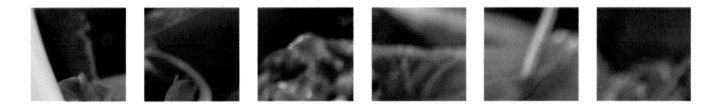

These tasty light meals are quick and easy to make – some are also ideal for making healthy packed lunches. They provide a filling meal and should stop you reaching for those unhealthy snacks between meals. If you do feel peckish, choose healthier snacks such as a piece of fruit, breadsticks, a currant bun, strips of vegetables with a low-fat dip, or salt- and sugar-free homemade popcorn.

serves 6

Winter Warmer Red Lentil Soup

Ingredients

225 g/8 oz dried red split lentils

1 red onion, diced

2 large carrots, sliced

1 celery stick, sliced

1 parsnip, diced

1 garlic clove, crushed

1.2 litres/2 pints vegetable stock

2 tsp paprika

freshly ground black pepper

1 tbsp snipped fresh chives, to garnish

To serve

6 tbsp low-fat natural fromage frais (optional)

crusty wholemeal or white bread

Nutritional Fact

Lentils contain good levels of B vitamins, which are thought to stop the build-up of a substance called homocysteine that can build up in the body and cause damage to the heart.

Serving Analysis

- Calories   87
- Protein   4.4g
- Carbohydrate   18g
- Sugars   5g
- Fat   0.4g
- Saturates   0.07g

1 Put the lentils, onion, vegetables, garlic, stock and paprika into a large saucepan. Bring to the boil and boil rapidly for 10 minutes. Reduce the heat, cover and simmer for 20 minutes, or until the lentils and vegetables are tender.

2 Leave the soup to cool slightly, then purée in small batches in a food processor or blender. Process until the mixture is smooth.

3 Return the soup to the saucepan and heat through thoroughly. Season to taste with pepper.

4 To serve, ladle the soup into warmed bowls and swirl in a tablespoonful of fromage frais, if desired. Sprinkle the chives over the soup to garnish and serve immediately with crusty bread.

serves 6

Speedy Broccoli Soup

Ingredients

350 g/12 oz broccoli

1 leek, sliced

1 celery stick, sliced

1 garlic clove, crushed

350 g/12 oz potato, diced

1 litre/1³/₄ pints vegetable stock

1 bay leaf

freshly ground black pepper

crusty bread or toasted croûtons, to serve

Nutritional Fact
Broccoli is a source of vitamins B₃ and B₅, both of which are thought to raise good cholesterol levels in the blood, and therefore help to balance good and bad cholesterol levels.

Serving Analysis
- Calories   140
- Protein   5.6g
- Carbohydrate   29g
- Sugars   3.6g
- Fat   1.3g
- Saturates   0.27g

1 Cut the broccoli into florets and set aside. Cut the thicker broccoli stalks into 1-cm/¹/₂-inch dice and put into a large saucepan with the leek, celery, garlic, potato, stock and bay leaf. Bring to the boil, then reduce the heat, cover and simmer for 15 minutes

2 Add the broccoli florets to the soup and return to the boil. Reduce the heat, cover and simmer for a further 3–5 minutes, or until the potato and broccoli stalks are tender.

3 Remove from the heat and leave the soup to cool slightly. Remove and discard the bay leaf. Purée the soup, in small batches, in a food processor or blender until smooth.

4 Return the soup to the saucepan and heat through thoroughly. Season to taste with pepper. Ladle the soup into warmed bowls and serve immediately with crusty bread or toasted croûtons.

serves 6

Chunky Vegetable Soup

Ingredients

2 carrots, sliced

1 onion, diced

1 garlic clove, crushed

350 g/12 oz new potatoes, diced

2 celery sticks, sliced

115 g/4 oz closed-cup mushrooms, quartered

400 g/14 oz canned chopped tomatoes in tomato juice

600 ml/1 pint vegetable stock

1 bay leaf

1 tsp dried mixed herbs or 1 tbsp chopped fresh mixed herbs

85 g/3 oz sweetcorn kernels, frozen or canned, drained

55 g/2 oz green cabbage, shredded

freshly ground black pepper

few sprigs of fresh basil, to garnish (optional)

crusty wholemeal or white bread rolls, to serve

Nutritional Fact

This dish can help you to achieve the target of five portions of vegetables you should aim for daily, which is crucial to a healthy heart.

Serving Analysis

• Calories	179
• Protein	5.4g
• Carbohydrate	34g
• Sugars	6g
• Fat	1.7g
• Saturates	0.07g

1 Put the carrots, onion, garlic, potatoes, celery, mushrooms, tomatoes and stock into a large saucepan. Stir in the bay leaf and herbs. Bring to the boil, then reduce the heat, cover and simmer for 25 minutes.

2 Add the sweetcorn and cabbage and return to the boil. Reduce the heat, cover and simmer for 5 minutes, or until the vegetables are tender. Remove and discard the bay leaf. Season to taste with pepper.

3 Ladle into warmed bowls and garnish with basil. Serve immediately with crusty bread rolls.

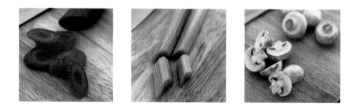

serves 4

Quick Mackerel Pâté

Ingredients

250 g/9 oz skinless smoked mackerel fillets

150 g/5^1/2 oz low-fat natural yogurt

1 tbsp chopped fresh parsley

1 tbsp lemon juice

finely grated rind of ^{1}/2 lemon

freshly ground black pepper

To garnish

4 lemon wedges

few sprigs of fresh parsley

To serve

1 red pepper, deseeded and cut into chunky strips

1 yellow pepper, deseeded and cut into chunky strips

2 carrots, cut into strips

2 celery sticks, cut into strips

slices wholemeal or white bread, toasted and cut into triangles

Nutritional Fact

Mackerel is an oily fish and a very rich source of omega-3 oils. These oils are excellent for helping to keep the heart healthy.

Serving Analysis

- Calories   190
- Protein   17g
- Carbohydrate   3.4g
- Sugars   2.9g
- Fat   11.7g
- Saturates   2.9g

1 Remove and discard any remaining bones from the mackerel fillets and put the fish into a small bowl. Mash the fish with a fork and combine with the yogurt, parsley and lemon juice and rind. Season to taste with pepper.

2 Divide the pâté between 4 ramekins. Cover and refrigerate until required or serve immediately.

3 To serve, garnish the pâté with lemon wedges and parsley sprigs and serve with the prepared vegetables and toasted bread.

serves 4

Raisin Coleslaw & Tuna-filled Pitta Breads

Ingredients

85 g/3 oz grated carrot

55 g/2 oz white cabbage, thinly sliced

85 g/3 oz low-fat natural yogurt

1 tsp cider vinegar

25 g/1 oz raisins

200 g/7 oz canned tuna steak in water, drained

2 tbsp pumpkin seeds

freshly ground black pepper

4 wholemeal or white pitta breads

4 dessert apples, to serve

Nutritional Fact

Pumpkin seeds contain omega-3 oils and omega-6 oils, both of which are thought to be beneficial to the heart.

Serving Analysis

• Calories	351
• Protein	21g
• Carbohydrate	59g
• Sugars	21g
• Fat	5.3g
• Saturates	1.6g

1 Mix the carrot, cabbage, yogurt, vinegar and raisins together in a bowl. Lightly stir in the tuna and half the pumpkin seeds and season to taste with pepper.

2 Lightly toast the pitta breads under a preheated hot grill or in a toaster, then leave to cool slightly. Using a sharp knife, cut each pitta bread in half. Divide the filling evenly between the pitta breads and sprinkle the remaining pumpkin seeds over the filling. Core and cut the apples into wedges, then serve immediately with the filled pitta breads.

serves 4

Salmon & Avocado Salad

Ingredients

450 g/1 lb new potatoes

4 salmon steaks, about 115 g/
4 oz each

1 avocado

juice of 1/2 lemon

55 g/2 oz baby spinach leaves

125 g/4 1/2 oz mixed small salad leaves,
including watercress

12 cherry tomatoes, halved

55 g/2 oz chopped walnuts

For the dressing

3 tbsp unsweetened clear apple juice

1 tsp balsamic vinegar

freshly ground black pepper

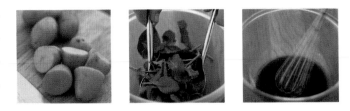

1 Cut the new potatoes into bite-sized pieces, put into a saucepan and cover with cold water. Bring to the boil, then reduce the heat, cover and simmer for 10–15 minutes, or until just tender. Drain and keep warm.

2 Meanwhile, preheat the grill to medium. Cook the salmon steaks under the preheated grill for 10–15 minutes, depending on the thickness of the steaks, turning halfway through cooking. Remove from the grill and keep warm.

3 While the potatoes and salmon are cooking, cut the avocado in half, remove and discard the stone and peel the flesh. Cut the avocado flesh into slices and coat in the lemon juice to prevent it from discolouring.

4 Toss the spinach leaves and mixed salad leaves together in a large serving bowl until combined. Arrange 6 cherry tomato halves on each plate of salad.

5 Remove and discard the skin and any bones from the salmon. Flake the salmon and divide between the plates along with the potatoes. Sprinkle the walnuts over the salads.

6 To make the dressing, mix the apple juice and vinegar together in a small bowl or jug and season well with pepper. Drizzle over the salads and serve immediately.

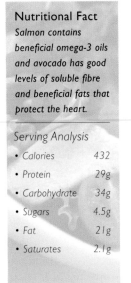

Nutritional Fact
Salmon contains beneficial omega-3 oils and avocado has good levels of soluble fibre and beneficial fats that protect the heart.

Serving Analysis
- *Calories*   432
- *Protein*   29g
- *Carbohydrate*   34g
- *Sugars*   4.5g
- *Fat*   21g
- *Saturates*   2.1g

serves 4

Chicken Wraps

Ingredients

150 g/5¹/₂ oz low-fat natural yogurt

1 tbsp wholegrain mustard

freshly ground black pepper

280 g/10 oz cooked skinless, boneless chicken breast, diced

140 g/5 oz iceberg lettuce, finely shredded

85 g/3 oz cucumber, thinly sliced

2 celery sticks, sliced

85 g/3 oz black seedless grapes, halved

8 × 20-cm/8-inch soft flour tortillas or 4 × 25-cm/10-inch soft flour tortillas

Nutritional Fact
Chicken is a good source of complete protein, without too much saturated fat. This means that it provides the building blocks for healthy cells, including the heart cells.

Serving Analysis

- *Calories* — 269
- *Protein* — 26.5g
- *Carbohydrate* — 34g
- *Sugars* — 7.2g
- *Fat* — 2.6g
- *Saturates* — 0.7g

1 Combine the yogurt and mustard in a bowl and season to taste with pepper. Stir in the chicken and toss until thoroughly coated.

2 Put the lettuce, cucumber, celery and grapes into a separate bowl and mix well.

3 Fold a tortilla in half and in half again to make a cone that is easy to hold. Half-fill the tortilla pocket with the salad mixture and top with some of the chicken mixture. Repeat with the remaining tortillas, salad and chicken. Serve immediately.

makes 9

Onion & Red Pepper Scones

Ingredients

sunflower oil, for oiling

175 g/6 oz self-raising white flour, plus extra for dusting

55 g/2 oz self-raising wholemeal flour

freshly ground black pepper

55 g/2 oz polyunsaturated spread

55 g/2 oz red onion, finely diced

55 g/2 oz red pepper, deseeded and finely diced

125 ml/4 fl oz skimmed or semi-skimmed milk, plus extra for dusting

mixed leaf salad, to serve

1 Preheat the oven to 230°C/450°F/Gas Mark 8. Very lightly oil a baking sheet.

2 Combine the flours in a mixing bowl and season with pepper. Rub in the spread with your fingertips until the mixture resembles fine breadcrumbs.

3 Stir in the onion and red pepper, then just enough milk to form a soft but not sticky dough.

4 Roll out the dough on a lightly floured work surface to a square about 2-cm/^{3}/$_4$-inch thick. Using a sharp knife, cut into 9 equal squares.

5 Arrange the scones on the prepared baking sheet, leaving a little room for them to rise and spread. Brush the surface with a little milk and bake in the preheated oven for 12–15 minutes, or until well risen and browned.

6 Remove from the oven and serve warm with a mixed leaf salad. These scones are best eaten on the day they are made – any leftover scones should be stored in an airtight container and consumed within 24 hours.

Nutritional Fact

Onion contains a substance called quercetin, which has been shown to help the heart stay healthy. It is also found in apple skins and green tea.

Serving Analysis

- Calories   149
- Protein   3.2g
- Carbohydrate   20g
- Sugars   1.6g
- Fat   6.3g
- Saturates   1.2g

Fish, Meat & Poultry

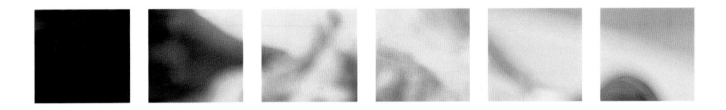

Using lean cuts of meat, removing the skin from poultry and increasing our consumption of fish are good ways to reduce the saturated fat content of our meals without compromising on the taste. These recipes demonstrate healthier ways to cook meat and fish dishes and suggest tasty accompaniments such as pasta, noodles, rice, couscous, bread, salads and seasonal vegetables.

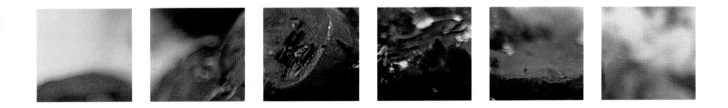

serves 4

Smoked Haddock with Tagliatelle Verde

Ingredients

450 g/1 lb smoked haddock fillets

280 g/10 oz dried tagliatelle verde

600 ml/1 pint skimmed or semi-skimmed milk

25 g/1 oz cornflour

2 shallots, finely chopped

2 tbsp snipped fresh chives

freshly ground black pepper

sliced tomatoes, to serve

1 Using a sharp knife, remove and discard the skin from the haddock fillets. Cut the fish into chunks, removing any remaining bones.

2 Bring a large saucepan of water to the boil, add the tagliatelle and return to the boil. Cook for 8–10 minutes, or until just tender.

3 Meanwhile, blend 125 ml/4 fl oz of the milk with the cornflour in a heatproof 850-ml/1 1/2-pint bowl. Place the remaining milk in a saucepan with the shallots and bring to the boil. Pour the boiling milk over the cornflour mixture, stirring constantly. Return the milk to the saucepan and bring back to the boil, stirring constantly, until the sauce thickens.

4 Stir the fish into the sauce, reduce the heat to low and gently simmer for 5 minutes, or until the fish is cooked. Stir in half of the chives.

5 Drain the tagliatelle and return to the saucepan, stir in the haddock sauce and season to taste with pepper. Serve immediately, garnished with the remaining chives and accompanied by sliced tomatoes.

Nutritional Fact

Haddock, although not an oily fish, is an excellent source of vitamin A, which is an antioxidant nutrient and therefore protects the heart against damage.

Serving Analysis

- *Calories*   48
- *Protein*   39g
- *Carbohydrate*   48g
- *Sugars*   6.7g
- *Fat*   12g
- *Saturates*   4.5g

serves 4

Grilled Tuna & Vegetable Kebabs

Ingredients

4 tuna steaks, about 140 g/5 oz each

2 red onions

12 cherry tomatoes

1 red pepper, deseeded and diced into 2.5-cm/1-inch pieces

1 yellow pepper, deseeded and diced into 2.5-cm/1-inch pieces

1 courgette, sliced

1 tbsp chopped fresh oregano

4 tbsp olive oil

freshly ground black pepper

lime wedges, to garnish

To serve

selection of salads

cooked couscous, new potatoes or bread

Nutritional Fact
It is important to eat many different fruit and vegetables to provide good levels of potassium to help lower high blood pressure and prevent heart disease.

Serving Analysis
- *Calories*   371
- *Protein*   35g
- *Carbohydrate*   15g
- *Sugars*   7.7g
- *Fat*   20g
- *Saturates*   0.08g

1 Preheat the grill to high. Cut the tuna into 2.5-cm/1-inch dice. Peel the onions, leaving the root intact and cut each onion lengthways into 6 wedges.

2 Divide the fish and vegetables evenly between 8 wooden skewers (presoaked to avoid burning) and arrange on the grill pan.

3 Mix the oregano and oil together in a small bowl. Season to taste with pepper. Lightly brush the kebabs with the oil and cook under the preheated grill for 10–15 minutes or until evenly cooked, turning occasionally. If you cannot fit all the kebabs on the grill pan at once, cook them in batches, keeping the cooked kebabs warm while cooking the remainder. Alternatively, these kebabs can be cooked on a barbecue.

4 Garnish with lime wedges and serve with a selection of salads, cooked couscous, new potatoes or bread.

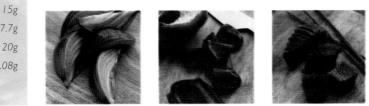

serves 4

Baked Lemon Cod

Nutritional Fact

White fish, such as cod and plaice, is low in saturated fat and high in protein that is essential for healthy building and repair of the body's cells.

Serving Analysis

• Calories	121
• Protein	25g
• Carbohydrate	2.6g
• Sugars	1.2g
• Fat	1.3g
• Saturates	0.02g

Ingredients

115 g/4 oz cucumber

2 celery sticks

4 thick cod fillets, about 140 g/5 oz each

1 tbsp chopped fresh parsley

grated rind and juice of 1 lemon

freshly ground black pepper

lemon wedges, to garnish

boiled new potatoes, lightly cooked seasonal vegetables or salads, to serve

1 Preheat the oven to 200°C/400°F/Gas Mark 6. Cut the cucumber and celery into long fine matchsticks and scatter over the base of an ovenproof dish that is large enough to fit the cod fillets in a single layer.

2 Arrange the cod fillets on the cucumber and celery and sprinkle the parsley, lemon rind and juice over the fillets. Season with pepper. Cover the dish with an ovenproof lid or foil and bake in the preheated oven for about 20 minutes, depending on the thickness of the fillets, until the flesh turns white and flakes easily.

3 Transfer the fish to a warmed serving plate with the cucumber and celery and spoon over the cooking juices. Garnish with lemon wedges and serve immediately with boiled new potatoes, seasonal vegetables or salads.

serves 4

Teriyaki Salmon Fillets with Chinese Noodles

Ingredients

4 salmon fillets, about 200 g/7 oz each

125 ml/4 fl oz teriyaki marinade

1 shallot, sliced

2-cm/³/₄-inch piece fresh root ginger, finely chopped

2 carrots, sliced

115 g/4 oz closed-cup mushrooms, sliced

1.2 litres/2 pints vegetable stock

250 g/9 oz dried medium egg noodles

115 g/4 oz frozen peas

175 g/6 oz Chinese leaves, shredded

4 spring onions, sliced

1 Wipe off any fish scales from the salmon skin. Arrange the salmon fillets, skin-side up, in a dish just large enough to fit them in a single layer. Mix the teriyaki marinade with the shallot and ginger in a small bowl and pour over the salmon. Cover and leave to marinate in the refrigerator for at least 1 hour, turning the salmon over halfway through the marinating time.

2 Put the carrots, mushrooms and stock into a large saucepan. Arrange the salmon, skin-side down, on a shallow baking tray. Pour the fish marinade into the saucepan of vegetables and stock and bring to the boil. Reduce the heat, cover and simmer for 10 minutes.

3 Meanwhile, preheat the grill to medium. Cook the salmon under the preheated grill for 10–15 minutes, depending on the thickness of the fillets, until the flesh turns pink and flakes easily. Remove from the grill and keep warm.

4 Add the noodles and peas to the stock and return to the boil. Reduce the heat, cover and simmer for 5 minutes, or until the noodles are tender. Stir in the Chinese leaves and spring onions and heat through for 1 minute.

5 Carefully drain off 300 ml/10 fl oz of the stock into a small heatproof jug and reserve. Drain and discard the remaining stock. Divide the noodles and vegetables between 4 warmed serving bowls and top each with a salmon fillet. Pour the reserved stock over each meal and serve immediately.

Nutritional Fact
Peas are legumes, not vegetables, and provide good protective levels of B vitamins and soluble fibre; they even retain these when frozen.

Serving Analysis
- Calories   533
- Protein   49g
- Carbohydrate   34.7g
- Sugars   13g
- Fat   22.4g
- Saturates   5.7g

serves 4

Boeuf Bourguignonne

Ingredients

400 g/14 oz lean beef

2 low-salt lean smoked back bacon rashers

12 shallots, peeled

1 garlic clove, crushed

225 g/8 oz closed-cup mushrooms, sliced

300 ml/10 fl oz red wine

425 ml/15 fl oz beef stock

2 bay leaves

2 tbsp chopped fresh thyme

55 g/2 oz cornflour

100 ml/3½ fl oz cold water

freshly ground black pepper

To serve

boiled brown or white rice

lightly cooked seasonal vegetables

Nutritional Fact

Choosing brown rice instead of white can help to increase your intake of insoluble fibre and B vitamins and clean toxins out of your system.

Serving Analysis

• Calories	376
• Protein	35g
• Carbohydrate	20g
• Sugars	1.6g
• Fat	11g
• Saturates	4.1g

1 Trim any visible fat from the beef and bacon and cut the meat into bite-sized pieces. Put the meat into a large saucepan with the shallots, garlic, mushrooms, wine, stock, bay leaves and 1 tablespoon of the thyme. Bring to the boil, then reduce the heat, cover and simmer for 50 minutes, or until the meat and shallots are tender.

2 Blend the cornflour with the water in a small bowl and stir into the casserole. Return to the boil, stirring constantly, and cook until the casserole thickens. Reduce the heat and simmer for a further 5 minutes. Season to taste with pepper.

3 Remove and discard the bay leaves. Transfer the boeuf bourguignonne to a warmed casserole dish and sprinkle over the remaining thyme. Serve with boiled rice and seasonal vegetables.

serves 4

Moroccan-style Turkey with Apricots

1 Put the turkey, onion, cumin, cinnamon, chilli pepper sauce, chickpeas and stock into a large saucepan and bring to the boil, then reduce the heat, cover and simmer for 15 minutes.

2 Stir in the apricots and return to the boil. Reduce the heat, cover and simmer for a further 15 minutes, or until the turkey is thoroughly cooked and tender.

3 Blend the cornflour with the water in a small bowl and stir into the casserole. Return to the boil, stirring constantly, and cook until the casserole thickens. Reduce the heat, cover and simmer for a further 5 minutes.

4 Stir half the coriander into the casserole. Transfer to a warmed serving dish and sprinkle over the remaining coriander. Serve immediately with cooked couscous, rice or jacket sweet potatoes.

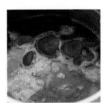

Nutritional Fact
Cumin has been traditionally used for centuries in the East as a heart tonic as it stimulates the circulation; it also helps digestion.

Serving Analysis

* *Calories* — 387
* *Protein* — 26g
* *Carbohydrate* — 63g
* *Sugars* — 36g
* *Fat* — 4.7g
* *Saturates* — 1.3g

Ingredients

400 g/14 oz skinless, boneless turkey breast, diced

1 onion, sliced

1 tsp ground cumin

1/2 tsp ground cinnamon

1 tsp hot chilli pepper sauce

240 g/8 1/2 oz canned chickpeas, drained

600 ml/1 pint chicken stock

12 dried apricots

40 g/1 1/2 oz cornflour

75 ml/2 1/2 fl oz cold water

2 tbsp chopped fresh coriander

cooked couscous, rice or jacket sweet potatoes, to serve

serves 4

Chicken Jambalaya

Ingredients

400 g/14 oz skinless, boneless chicken breast, diced

1 red onion, diced

1 garlic clove, crushed

600 ml/1 pint chicken stock

400 g/14 oz canned chopped tomatoes in tomato juice

280 g/10 oz brown rice

1–2 tsp hot chilli powder

1/2 tsp paprika

1 tsp dried oregano

1 red pepper, deseeded and diced

1 yellow pepper, deseeded and diced

85 g/3 oz frozen sweetcorn kernels

85 g/3 oz frozen peas

3 tbsp chopped fresh parsley

freshly ground black pepper

crisp green salad, to serve

  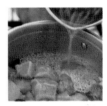

Nutritional Fact

Garlic is an important ingredient for a healthy heart. Its active component, allicin, helps to stimulate circulation and keep blood thin to prevent heart disease.

Serving Analysis

• Calories	309
• Protein	34.5g
• Carbohydrate	36g
• Sugars	8.3g
• Fat	3.4g
• Saturates	0.2g

1 Put the chicken, onion, garlic, stock, tomatoes and rice into a large, heavy-based saucepan. Add the chilli powder, paprika and oregano and stir well. Bring to the boil, then reduce the heat, cover and simmer for 25 minutes.

2 Add the red and yellow peppers, sweetcorn and peas to the rice mixture and return to the boil. Reduce the heat, cover and simmer for a further 10 minutes, or until the rice is just tender (brown rice retains a 'nutty' texture when cooked) and most of the stock has been absorbed but is not completely dry.

3 Stir in 2 tablespoons of the parsley and season to taste with pepper. Transfer the jambalaya to a warmed serving dish, garnish with the remaining parsley and serve with a crisp green salad.

serves 4

Sticky Lime Chicken

1 Preheat the oven to 190°C/375°F/Gas Mark 5. Arrange the chicken breasts in a shallow roasting tin.

2 Put the lime rind and juice, honey, oil, garlic, if using, and thyme in a small bowl and combine thoroughly. Spoon the mixture evenly over the chicken breasts and season with pepper.

3 Roast the chicken in the preheated oven, basting every 10 minutes, for 35–40 minutes, or until the chicken is tender and the juices run clear when a skewer is inserted into the thickest part of the meat. If the juices still run pink, return the chicken to the oven and cook for a further 5 minutes, then re-test. As the chicken cooks the liquid in the pan thickens to give the tasty sticky coating.

4 Serve with boiled new potatoes and seasonal vegetables.

Ingredients

4 part-boned, skinless chicken breasts, about 140 g/5 oz each

grated rind and juice of 1 lime

1 tbsp clear honey

1 tbsp olive oil

1 garlic clove, chopped (optional)

1 tbsp chopped fresh thyme

freshly ground black pepper

To serve

boiled new potatoes

lightly cooked seasonal vegetables

Nutritional Fact
Removing the skin from the chicken gets rid of most of the saturated fat.

Serving Analysis
- *Calories*   203
- *Protein*   32.5g
- *Carbohydrate*   5.3g
- *Sugars*   4.4g
- *Fat*   5.3g
- *Saturates*   1g

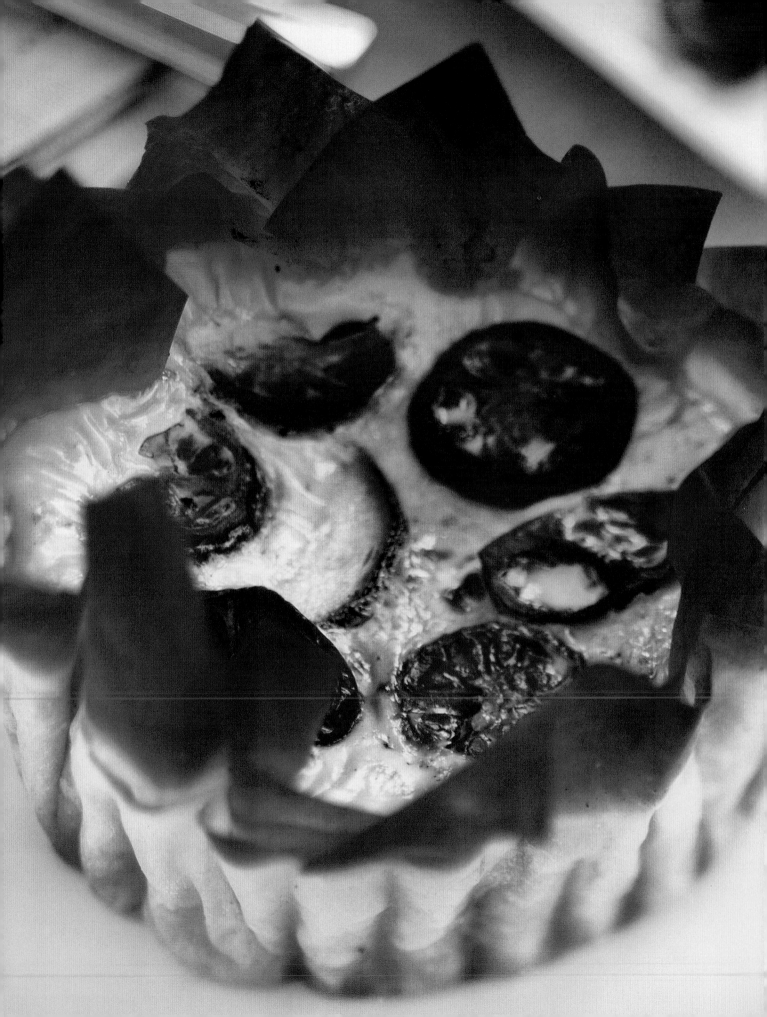

Vegetarian

You don't have to be a vegetarian to enjoy the delicious
recipes in this chapter. The variety of flavours and textures
featured in the selection of vegetables available today
makes a delightful change from meat-based recipes. Fresh
chillies, herbs and ginger and oriental spices are just some of
the ingredients used to enhance these easy-to-make meals.

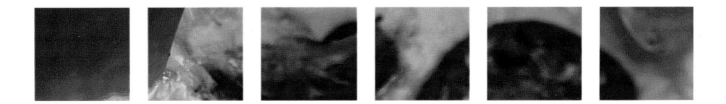

serves 4

Roasted Vegetables with Hot Chilli Pepper Dip

Ingredients

4 tbsp olive oil

2 potatoes, about 175 g/6 oz each

2 red-fleshed sweet potatoes, about 175 g/6 oz each

1 large parsnip

6 turnips, about 85 g/3 oz each

few sprigs of fresh rosemary

2 garlic cloves, crushed

2 courgettes

1 aubergine

For the dip

3 fresh red chillies, sliced

1 red pepper, deseeded and finely diced

1 onion, finely chopped

400 g/14 oz canned chopped tomatoes in tomato juice

100 ml/3 1/2 fl oz vegetable stock or cold water

1 Preheat the oven to 220°C/425°F/Gas Mark 7. Divide the oil between 2 large roasting tins and heat in the oven.

2 Scrub the potatoes and cut into wedges. Peel the parsnip and turnips. Cut the parsnip into strips about the same size as the potato wedges. Cut the turnips in half. Cook in a large saucepan of boiling water for 5 minutes, drain well and carefully add to the roasting tins. Using a spoon, turn and coat the vegetables with the hot oil. Divide the rosemary and garlic between the roasting tins and roast in the preheated oven for 15 minutes.

3 Cut the courgettes and aubergine into long chunks, just slightly larger than the potato wedges. Remove the roasting tins from the oven and divide the courgettes and aubergine between them, carefully tossing them in the hot oil. Roast for a further 45 minutes–1 hour, turning occasionally so that they roast evenly.

4 Meanwhile, make the dip. Reserve a few chilli slices for garnish and put the remainder into a saucepan with all the remaining dip ingredients. Bring to the boil, then reduce the heat, cover and simmer for 20 minutes until the onion is tender. Leave the dip to cool for 15 minutes, then process in a food processor or blender in small batches, until smooth. Return the dip to the saucepan and heat through thoroughly just prior to serving.

5 Pour the dip into 4 individual serving dishes, garnish with the reserved chilli slices. Divide the roasted vegetables between warmed serving plates. Serve immediately.

Nutritional Fact

Roasting vegetables in olive oil is much healthier than using saturated lard or butter.

Serving Analysis

- Calories · · · · 443
- Protein · · · · 9.7g
- Carbohydrate · · · · 74g
- Sugars · · · · 26.5g
- Fat · · · · 15g
- Saturates · · · · 0.2g

serves 4

Mushroom Stroganoff

Ingredients

550 g/1 lb 4 oz mixed fresh mushrooms, such as chestnut, chanterelles, ceps and oyster

1 red onion, diced

2 garlic cloves, crushed

425 ml/15 fl oz vegetable stock

1 tbsp tomato purée

2 tbsp lemon juice

15 g/¹/₂ oz cornflour

2 tbsp cold water

115 g/4 oz low-fat natural yogurt

3 tbsp chopped fresh parsley

freshly ground black pepper

To serve

boiled brown or white rice

crisp green salad

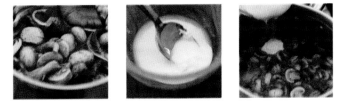

Nutritional Fact

Mushrooms have long been eaten to promote health and vitality and are said to enhance the body's adaptive capacity to fight disease and strengthen itself.

Serving Analysis

- Calories   87
- Protein   5.1g
- Carbohydrate   16.8g
- Sugars   4.4g
- Fat   1.2g
- Saturates   0.4g

1 Put the mushrooms, onion, garlic, stock, tomato purée and lemon juice into a saucepan and bring to the boil. Reduce the heat, cover and simmer for 15 minutes, or until the onion is tender.

2 Blend the cornflour with the water in a small bowl and stir into the mushroom mixture. Return to the boil, stirring constantly, and cook until the sauce thickens. Reduce the heat and simmer for a further 2–3 minutes, stirring occasionally.

3 Just before serving, remove the saucepan from the heat and stir in the yogurt, making sure that the stroganoff is not boiling or it may separate and curdle. Stir in 2 tablespoons of the parsley and season to taste with pepper. Transfer the stroganoff to a warmed serving dish, sprinkle over the remaining parsley and serve immediately with boiled brown or white rice and a crisp green salad.

serves 4

Toasted Pine Kernel & Vegetable Couscous

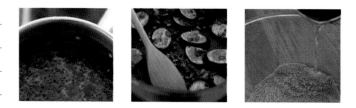

Ingredients

115 g/4 oz dried green lentils
55 g/2 oz pine kernels
1 tbsp olive oil
1 onion, diced
2 garlic cloves, crushed
280 g/10 oz courgettes, sliced
250 g/9 oz tomatoes, chopped
400 g/14 oz canned artichoke hearts, drained and cut in half lengthways
250 g/9 oz couscous
450 ml/16 fl oz vegetable stock
3 tbsp torn fresh basil leaves, plus extra leaves to garnish
freshly ground black pepper

1 Put the lentils into a saucepan with plenty of cold water, bring to the boil and boil rapidly for 10 minutes. Reduce the heat, cover and simmer for a further 15 minutes, or until tender.

2 Meanwhile, preheat the grill to medium. Spread the pine kernels out in a single layer on a baking sheet and toast under the preheated grill, turning to brown evenly – watch constantly as they brown very quickly. Tip the pine kernels into a small dish and set aside.

3 Heat the oil in a non-stick frying pan over a medium heat, add the onion, garlic and courgettes and cook, stirring frequently, for 8–10 minutes, or until tender and the courgettes have browned slightly. Add the tomatoes and artichoke halves and heat through thoroughly for 5 minutes.

4 Meanwhile, put the couscous into a heatproof bowl. Bring the stock to the boil in a saucepan and pour over the couscous, cover and leave for 10 minutes until the couscous absorbs the stock and becomes tender.

5 Drain the lentils and stir into the couscous. Stir in the torn basil leaves and season well with pepper. Transfer the couscous to a warmed serving dish and spoon over the cooked vegetables. Sprinkle the pine kernels over the top of the vegetables and couscous, garnish with basil leaves and serve immediately.

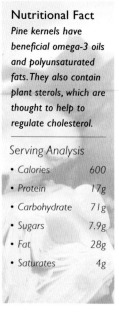

Nutritional Fact

Pine kernels have beneficial omega-3 oils and polyunsaturated fats. They also contain plant sterols, which are thought to help to regulate cholesterol.

Serving Analysis

• Calories	600
• Protein	17g
• Carbohydrate	71g
• Sugars	7.9g
• Fat	28g
• Saturates	4g

serves 4

Tomato, Courgette & Basil Filo Tartlets

Nutritional Fact

Eggs contain good levels of iron, which is essential for healthy red blood cells. They also contain vitamins B_6 and B_{12}, which are thought to help prevent arteries furring up.

Serving Analysis

• Calories	232
• Protein	7g
• Carbohydrate	18.7g
• Sugars	5.8g
• Fat	14.8g
• Saturates	3.7g

1 Preheat the oven to 190°C/375°F/Gas Mark 5. Lightly oil 4 × 12-cm/4^1/2-inch individual loose-bottomed flan tins.

2 Working quickly so that the filo pastry does not dry out, cut each sheet into 6 equal-sized pieces measuring about 16 × 14 cm/6^1/4 × 5^1/2 inches. Layer 3 pieces of pastry at a time in the 4 flan tins, lightly brushing between each layer with oil. Carefully press the pastry into the sides of the tins so that the corners of the pastry squares point upwards. Arrange the tins on a large baking sheet.

3 Sprinkle two-thirds of the torn basil leaves over the pastry bases and cover with overlapping slices of tomato and courgette. Beat the eggs with the milk in a bowl and season well with pepper. Divide the egg mixture evenly between the tins and sprinkle the remaining torn basil leaves over it.

4 Bake in the preheated oven for 20–25 minutes, or until the egg mixture has set and the pastry is crisp and golden. Serve warm or cold, garnished with basil leaves and with a selection of salads and boiled new potatoes.

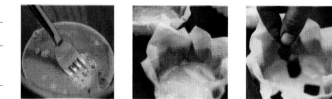

Ingredients

olive oil, for oiling and brushing

2 × 48- × 28-cm/19- × 11-inch sheets filo pastry

1 tbsp torn fresh basil leaves, plus extra leaves to garnish

7–8 cherry tomatoes, thinly sliced

1 courgette, thinly sliced

2 eggs, beaten

150 ml/5 fl oz skimmed or semi-skimmed milk

freshly ground black pepper

To serve

selection of salads

boiled new potatoes

serves 4

Sweetcorn & Green Bean-filled Jacket Sweet Potatoes

Ingredients

4 red-fleshed sweet potatoes, about 250 g/9 oz each

115 g/4 oz frozen broad beans

115 g/4 oz frozen sweetcorn kernels

115 g/4 oz fine long green beans

140 g/5 oz tomatoes

1 tbsp olive oil

1 tbsp balsamic vinegar

freshly ground black pepper

2 tbsp torn fresh basil leaves, plus extra leaves to garnish

Nutritional Fact

Sweetcorn is one of the few vegetables that has beneficial antioxidant properties that actually increase with cooking.

Serving Analysis

• Calories	362
• Protein	8g
• Carbohydrate	76g
• Sugars	28g
• Fat	4.2g
• Saturates	0.1g

1 Preheat the oven to 190°C/375°F/Gas Mark 5. Scrub the sweet potatoes and pierce the skin of each potato with a sharp knife several times. Arrange on a baking sheet and bake in the preheated oven for 1–1¼ hours, or until soft and tender when pierced with the point of a sharp knife. Keep warm.

2 When the potatoes are cooked, bring a saucepan of water to the boil, add the broad beans and sweetcorn and return to the boil. Reduce the heat, cover and simmer for 5 minutes. Trim the green beans, cut in half and add to the saucepan. Return to the boil, then reduce the heat, cover and simmer for 3 minutes, or until the green beans are just tender.

3 Blend the oil with the vinegar in a small bowl and season to taste with pepper. Drain the sweetcorn and beans, return to the saucepan, add the tomatoes and pour the dressing over. Add the torn basil leaves and mix well.

4 Remove the sweet potatoes from the oven, cut in half lengthways and open up. Divide the sweetcorn and bean filling between the potatoes and serve immediately, garnished with basil leaves.

serves 4–6

Chilli Beans

Ingredients

200 g/7 oz dried mixed beans, such as kidney, soya, pinto, cannellini and chickpeas

1 red onion, diced

1 garlic clove, crushed

1 tbsp hot chilli powder

400 g/14 oz canned chopped tomatoes in tomato juice

1 tbsp tomato purée

To serve

4 tbsp low-fat natural yogurt

jacket potatoes, boiled rice or soft flour tortilla wraps

Nutritional Fact

Cooking tomatoes actually increases the antioxidant activity of a substance called lycopene, which gives them their colour and protects the heart.

Serving Analysis

- Calories   53
- Protein   3.2g
- Carbohydrate   10g
- Sugars   4.3g
- Fat   0.5g
- Saturates   0.05g

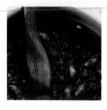

1 Soak the beans overnight or for 8 hours in a large bowl of cold water. Drain, rinse and put the beans into a large saucepan. Cover well with cold water, then bring to the boil and boil rapidly for 10 minutes. Reduce the heat, cover and simmer for a further 45 minutes, or until tender. Drain. (Alternatively, if time is short, use 450 g/1 lb drained and rinsed canned mixed beans and start at Step 2.)

2 Put the cooked beans, onion, garlic, chilli powder, tomatoes and tomato purée into a saucepan and bring to the boil. Reduce the heat, cover and simmer for 20–25 minutes, or until the onion is tender.

3 Serve each portion of the chilli beans with a tablespoon of the yogurt, accompanied by jacket potatoes, boiled rice or soft flour tortilla wraps.

serves 4

Curried Potato, Cauliflower & Spinach

Ingredients

2 tbsp olive oil

1 onion, diced

1 tbsp garam masala

$\frac{1}{2}$ tsp ground cumin

1 tsp ground turmeric

400 g/14 oz canned chopped tomatoes in tomato juice

300 ml/10 fl oz vegetable stock

450 g/1 lb new potatoes, cut into chunks

280 g/10 oz cauliflower florets

55 g/2 oz flaked almonds

250 g/9 oz baby spinach leaves

naan bread, to serve

1 Heat the oil in a saucepan over a medium–low heat, add the onion and spices and cook, stirring constantly, for 2–3 minutes, taking care not to burn the spices as they are cooking in a small amount of oil. Add the tomatoes and stock and bring to the boil, then reduce the heat, cover and simmer for 25 minutes.

2 Meanwhile, put the potatoes into a separate saucepan, cover with cold water and bring to the boil. Reduce the heat, cover and simmer for 15 minutes. Add the cauliflower and return to the boil, then reduce the heat, cover and simmer for a further 10 minutes, or until just tender.

3 While the vegetables are cooking, preheat the grill to medium. Spread the almonds out in a single layer on a baking sheet and toast under the preheated grill, turning to brown evenly, for 1–2 minutes – watch constantly as they brown very quickly. Tip the almonds into a small dish and set aside.

4 Add the spinach to the potatoes and cauliflower, stir into the water and simmer for 1 minute. Drain the vegetables and return to the saucepan. Stir in the curried tomato sauce. Transfer to a warmed serving dish, sprinkle over the toasted almonds and serve immediately with naan bread.

Nutritional Fact
Turmeric has been shown to lower cholesterol, prevent the formation of internal blood clots, improve circulation and may help to prevent heart disease and strokes.

Serving Analysis
- Calories   339
- Protein   11g
- Carbohydrate   43g
- Sugars   6.6g
- Fat   15.6g
- Saturates   1.7g

serves 4

Chinese Vegetables & Beansprouts with Noodles

Ingredients

1.2 litres/2 pints vegetable stock
1 garlic clove, crushed
1-cm/½-inch piece fresh root ginger, finely chopped
225 g/8 oz dried medium egg noodles
1 red pepper, deseeded and sliced
85 g/3 oz frozen peas
115 g/4 oz broccoli florets
85 g/3 oz shiitake mushrooms, sliced
2 tbsp sesame seeds
225 g/8 oz canned water chestnuts, drained and halved
225 g/8 oz canned bamboo shoots, drained
280 g/10 oz Chinese leaves, sliced
140 g/5 oz beansprouts
3 spring onions, sliced
1 tbsp dark soy sauce
freshly ground black pepper

1 Bring the stock, garlic and ginger to the boil in a large saucepan. Stir in the noodles, red pepper, peas, broccoli and mushrooms and return to the boil. Reduce the heat, cover and simmer for 5–6 minutes, or until the noodles are tender.

2 Meanwhile, preheat the grill to medium. Spread the sesame seeds out in a single layer on a baking sheet and toast under the preheated grill, turning to brown evenly – watch constantly as they brown very quickly. Tip the sesame seeds into a small dish and set aside.

3 Once the noodles are tender, add the water chestnuts, bamboo shoots, Chinese leaves, beansprouts and spring onions to the saucepan. Return the stock to the boil, stir to mix the ingredients and simmer for a further 2–3 minutes to heat through thoroughly.

4 Carefully drain off 300 ml/10 fl oz of the stock into a small heatproof jug and reserve. Drain and discard any remaining stock and turn the noodles and vegetables into a warmed serving dish. Quickly mix the soy sauce with the reserved stock and pour over the noodles and vegetables. Season to taste with pepper and serve immediately.

Nutritional Fact

It is thought that ginger may thin the blood and help to regulate cholesterol. It is also used as a digestive aid.

Serving Analysis

- Calories   336
- Protein   16g
- Carbohydrate   58g
- Sugars   4.4g
- Fat   5.8g
- Saturates   1g

Desserts & Baking

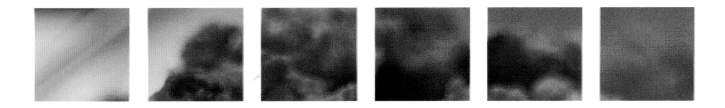

Many desserts and cakes are laden with fat and sugar – this is what makes them so tasty and yearned for! This chapter shows how traditional recipes such as crumbles, cheesecakes and flapjacks can be made healthier by reducing the fat and sugar content, but without cutting out the good taste factor. Desserts can also play an important part in helping to achieve the recommended five-a-day portions of fruit and vegetables.

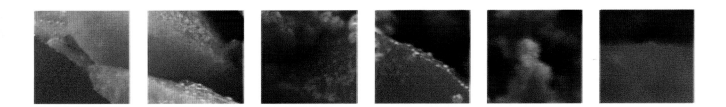

Nutritional Fact
Using cocoa powder rather than melted chocolate gives a good chocolate flavour without the high saturated fat and sugar content found in chocolate.

Serving Analysis

• *Calories*	*232*
• *Protein*	*6.4g*
• *Carbohydrate*	*42g*
• *Sugars*	*29g*
• *Fat*	*5.6g*
• *Saturates*	*1.9g*

serves 4–6

Chocolate Pear Roulade

Ingredients

sunflower oil, for oiling
40 g/1 1/2 oz plain flour
15 g/1/2 oz cocoa powder, plus 1 tsp for dusting
2 eggs
85 g/3 oz caster sugar
1 tbsp hot water
1 orange, halved
2 ripe pears
200 g/7 oz low-fat fromage frais

1 Preheat the oven to 200°C/400°F/Gas Mark 6. Line a 27- x 17-cm (10³/4- x 6¹/2-inch) Swiss roll tin with greaseproof paper and oil very lightly.

2 Sift the flour and cocoa powder together into a mixing bowl.

3 Put the eggs and sugar into a warmed, heatproof glass mixing bowl and whisk until pale in colour and a trail is left when the whisk is lifted out of the mixture. This will take approximately 15 minutes if using an electric hand mixer. (If using a manual hand mixer, the mixture can be whisked over a saucepan of hot but not boiling water to help reduce the whisking time.)

4 Carefully fold the flour mixture into the whisked egg mixture using a metal tablespoon. Stir in the hot water. Pour the mixture into the prepared tin and gently tilt to level the mixture. Bake in the preheated oven for 8–10 minutes, or until the point of a sharp knife inserted into the centre of the sponge comes out clean.

5 Turn the sponge out on to a sheet of greaseproof paper placed over a clean tea towel. Carefully peel the lining paper off the sponge and trim any crisp edges with a sharp knife.

6 Using the greaseproof paper under the sponge, loosely roll up the sponge from the short end and leave to cool completely on a wire rack.

7 Meanwhile, squeeze the juice from 1 orange half into a bowl. Peel, quarter and core the pears. Thinly slice and toss in the juice to prevent discolouration. Slice the remaining orange half and reserve for decoration.

8 Carefully unroll the cooled sponge and spread with the fromage frais, leaving a 2.5-cm/1-inch border. Drain any excess orange juice from the pears. Reserve a few pear slices for decoration and cover the fromage frais with the remaining slices. Carefully re-roll the sponge.

9 Using a sharp knife, slice the roulade into portions and serve on plates decorated with the reserved pear and orange slices. Lightly sift over the cocoa powder and serve immediately. This dessert is best eaten on the day it is made – any leftover roulade should be stored in the refrigerator and consumed within 24 hours.

serves 4–6

Peach & Apple Crumble

Ingredients

1 cooking apple
2 dessert apples
125 ml/4 fl oz cold water
400 g/14 oz canned peach slices in fruit juice, drained
85g/3 oz plain flour
55 g/2 oz porridge oats
55 g/2 oz demerara sugar
55 g/2 oz polyunsaturated spread
custard made with skimmed milk, low-fat natural fromage frais or yogurt, to serve

Nutritional Fact

Apples contain high levels of pectin, a type of fibre which is particularly good at carrying toxins out of the body. They also have good levels of potassium to aid heart health.

Serving Analysis

• Calories	315
• Protein	3.4g
• Carbohydrate	54g
• Sugars	32g
• Fat	9.9g
• Saturates	1.8g

1 Preheat the oven to 190°C/375°F/Gas Mark 5. Peel, core and slice the apples and put into a small saucepan with the water. Bring to the boil, then cover and simmer, stirring occasionally, for 4–5 minutes, or until just tender. Remove from the heat and drain away any excess liquid. Stir the drained peach slices into the apple and transfer the fruit to a 1-litre/1³⁄₄-pint ovenproof dish.

2 Meanwhile, combine the flour, oats and sugar in a mixing bowl. Rub in the spread with your fingertips until the mixture resembles fine breadcrumbs.

3 Sprinkle the crumble topping evenly over the fruit and bake in the preheated oven for 20 minutes, or until golden brown. Serve warm with custard made with skimmed milk, or low-fat natural fromage frais or yogurt. This dessert is best eaten on the day it is made – any leftover crumble should be stored in the refrigerator and consumed within 24 hours.

serves 4

Blueberry Fools

Ingredients

25 g/1 oz custard powder

300 ml/10 fl oz skimmed or semi-skimmed milk

2 tbsp caster sugar

150 g/5 1/2 oz fresh or frozen blueberries, thawed if frozen

200 g/7 oz low-fat natural fromage frais

1 Blend the custard powder with 50 ml/2 fl oz of the milk in a heatproof bowl. Bring the remaining milk to the boil in a small saucepan and pour over the custard mixture, mixing well. Return the custard to the saucepan and return to the boil over medium–low heat, stirring constantly, until thickened. Pour the custard into the bowl and sprinkle the sugar over the top of the custard to prevent a skin forming. Cover and leave to cool completely.

2 Reserve 12 blueberries for decoration. Put the remaining blueberries and cold custard into a blender and process until smooth.

3 Spoon the fromage frais and blueberry mixture in alternate layers into 4 tall glasses. Decorate with the reserved blueberries and serve immediately.

Nutritional Fact
Blueberries are rich in vitamin C, which is an antioxidant and may boost the immune system. They are also rich in anthocyanins, plant chemicals that help to promote heart health.

Serving Analysis
- Calories   133
- Protein   5.9g
- Carbohydrate   22g
- Sugars   20.6g
- Fat   2.8g
- Saturates   1.5g

serves 4

Exotic Fruit Cocktail

Nutritional Fact

Pineapple contains a substance called bromelain, which has been shown to reduce blood pressure effectively and help prevent heart disease.

Serving Analysis

- Calories   152
- Protein   2g
- Carbohydrate   38g
- Sugars   31.4g
- Fat   0.9g
- Saturates   0.1g

Ingredients

2 oranges

2 large passion fruit

1 pineapple

1 pomegranate

1 banana

1 Cut 1 orange in half and squeeze the juice into a bowl, discarding any pips. Using a sharp knife, cut away all the peel and pith from the second orange. Working over the bowl to catch the juice, carefully cut the orange segments between the membranes to obtain skinless segments of fruit. Discard any pips.

2 Cut the passion fruit in half, scoop the flesh into a nylon sieve and, using a spoon, push the pulp and juice into the bowl of orange segments. Discard the pips.

3 Using a sharp knife, cut away all the skin from the pineapple and cut the flesh lengthways into quarters. Cut away the central hard core. Cut the flesh into chunks and add to the orange and passion fruit mixture. Cover and refrigerate the fruit at this stage if you are not serving immediately.

4 Cut the pomegranate into quarters and, using your fingers or a teaspoon, remove the red seeds from the membrane. Cover and refrigerate until ready to serve – do not add too early to the fruit cocktail as the seeds discolour the other fruit.

5 Just before serving, peel and slice the banana, add to the fruit cocktail with the pomegranate seeds and mix thoroughly. Serve immediately.

serves 4

Grilled Cinnamon Oranges

Ingredients

4 large oranges

1 tsp ground cinnamon

1 tbsp demerara sugar

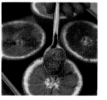

1 Preheat the grill to high. Cut the oranges in half and discard any pips. Using a sharp or curved grapefruit knife, carefully cut the flesh away from the skin by cutting around the edge of the fruit. Cut across the segments to loosen the flesh into bite-sized pieces that will spoon out easily.

2 Place the orange halves, cut-side up, in a shallow, heatproof dish. Mix the cinnamon with the sugar in a small bowl and sprinkle evenly over the orange halves. Cook under the preheated grill for 3–5 minutes, or until the sugar has caramelized and is golden and bubbling. Serve immediately.

Nutritional Fact

In Asian medicine, cinnamon has long been used to treat high blood pressure and poor blood circulation.

Serving Analysis

• Calories	72
• Protein	1.2g
• Carbohydrate	18g
• Sugars	14.7g
• Fat	0.2g
• Saturates	0.02g

makes 10

Apricot Flapjacks

Ingredients

sunflower oil, for oiling

175 g/6 oz polyunsaturated spread

85 g/3 oz demerara sugar

55 g/2 oz clear honey

140 g/5 oz dried apricots, chopped

2 tsp sesame seeds

225 g/8 oz porridge oats

1 Preheat the oven to 180°C/350°F/Gas Mark 4. Very lightly oil a 26- x 17-cm/ 10¹/₂- x 6¹/₂-inch shallow baking tin.

2 Put the spread, sugar and honey into a small saucepan over a low heat and heat until the ingredients have melted together – do not boil. When the ingredients are warm and well combined, stir in the apricots, sesame seeds and oats.

3 Spoon the mixture into the prepared tin and lightly level with the back of a spoon. Cook in the preheated oven for 20–25 minutes, or until golden brown. Remove from the oven, cut into 10 bars and leave to cool completely before removing from the baking tin. Store the flapjacks in an airtight tin and consume within 2–3 days.

Nutritional Fact

Oats are a fantastic source of slow-releasing energy. Sesame seeds contain omega oils that are important for heart health and cholesterol regulation.

Serving Analysis

• *Calories*	*293*
• *Protein*	*3.6g*
• *Carbohydrate*	*34g*
• *Sugars*	*20g*
• *Fat*	*16.5g*
• *Saturates*	*2.9g*

Makes one 450 g/1 lb loaf – 10–12 slices

Sultana Tealoaf

Ingredients

sunflower oil, for oiling

40 g/1½ oz bran flakes

115 g/4 oz sultanas

85 g/3 oz demerara sugar

300 ml/10 fl oz skimmed or semi-skimmed milk

200 g/7 oz self-raising flour

tea or freshly squeezed fruit juice, to serve

Nutritional Fact
Just 1 tablespoon of dried fruit counts as one of the five portions of fruit and vegetables recommended per day.

Serving Analysis

- *Calories*   156
- *Protein*   3.5g
- *Carbohydrate*   34g
- *Sugars*   16.6g
- *Fat*   1.3g
- *Saturates*   0.5g

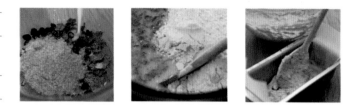

1 Very lightly oil a 450-g/1-lb loaf tin and line the base with greaseproof paper.

2 Put the bran flakes, sultanas, sugar and milk into a mixing bowl, cover and leave to soak for at least 1 hour in the refrigerator, or until the bran flakes have softened and the fruit has plumped up after absorbing some of the milk – the mixture can be left overnight in the refrigerator.

3 Preheat the oven to 190°C/375°F/Gas Mark 5. Stir the flour into the soaked ingredients, mix well and spoon into the loaf tin. Bake in the preheated oven for 40–45 minutes, or until the tip of a sharp knife inserted into the centre of the loaf comes out clean. Leave to cool in the tin on a wire rack.

4 When cold, turn the loaf out and discard the lining paper. Serve in slices with cups of tea or glasses of freshly squeezed fruit juice. Store any leftover loaf in an airtight container and consume within 2–3 days.

serves 4

Mango Cheesecakes

Ingredients

sunflower oil, for oiling
25 g/1 oz polyunsaturated spread
$^1/_2$ tsp ground ginger
55 g/2 oz porridge oats
1 large ripe mango, about 600 g/1 lb 5 oz
250 g/9 oz virtually fat-free quark soft cheese
100 g/3$^1/_2$ oz medium-fat soft cheese
12 raspberries, to decorate (optional)

1 Line the base and sides of 4 x 150-ml/5-fl oz ramekins with greaseproof paper and very lightly oil.

2 Melt the spread in a small saucepan over a low heat, remove from the heat and stir in the ginger and oats. Mix thoroughly and leave to cool.

3 Using a sharp knife, cut the mango lengthways down either side of the thin central stone. Peel the flesh. Cut away any flesh from around the stone and peel. Cut the flesh into chunks and reserve 115 g/4 oz. Put the remaining mango flesh into a food processor or blender and process until smooth. Transfer to a small bowl.

4 Drain away any excess fluid from the cheeses and, using a fork or tablespoon, blend together in a bowl. Finely chop the reserved mango flesh and stir into the cheese mixture along with 1 tablespoon of the mango purée. Divide the cheesecake filling evenly between the ramekins and level with the back of a spoon. Cover each cheesecake evenly with the cooled oat mixture and chill in the refrigerator for at least 3 hours for the filling to firm. Cover and refrigerate the mango purée.

5 To serve, carefully trim the lining paper level with the oat mixture. As the oat base is crumbly, place an individual serving plate on top of a ramekin when turning out the cheesecakes. Holding firmly, turn both over to invert. Carefully remove the ramekin and peel away the lining paper. Repeat for the remaining cheesecakes. Spoon the mango purée around each cheesecake and decorate the top of each with 3 raspberries, if using. Serve immediately.

> **Nutritional Fact**
> *Mangoes are a good source of fibre, beta-carotene and vitamin C. They are also thought to help aid digestion and cleanse the blood.*
>
> *Serving Analysis*
> * *Calories*   *259*
> * *Protein*   *14g*
> * *Carbohydrate*   *23g*
> * *Sugars*   *11.7g*
> * *Fat*   *12g*
> * *Saturates*   *3.8g*